# EMEKA'S GIFT

## An African Counting Story

## IFEOMA ONYEFULU

COBBLEHILL BOOKS

Dutton    New York

*To my parents Emmanuel and Emily, and to my son, Emeka,*
*for being a wonderful traveling companion.*

First published in the United States 1995 by Cobblehill Books,
an affiliate of Dutton Children's Books, a division of
Penguin Books USA Inc., 375 Hudson Street, New York, New York 10014

Originally published in Great Britain 1995 by Frances Lincoln Limited, London

Library of Congress Cataloging-in-Publication Data
Onyefulu, Ifeoma.
Emeka's gift : an African counting story / Ifeoma Onyefulu.   p. cm.
ISBN 0-525-65205-1
1. Africa—Social life and customs—Juvenile literature. 2. Counting—Juvenile
literature. I: Title: DT3.059  1995  960—dc20  94-30700  CIP  AC

Designed by Sonja Ferrier   Set in Perpetua
Printed and bound in Hong Kong

First American Edition   10 9 8 7 6 5 4 3 2 1

## A Note from the Author

Emeka, the little boy in this book, lives in a village called Ibaji, in southern Nigeria, and comes from a tribe called Igala. The Igala people, who speak the Kwa language, are traders, farmers, fishermen and healers.

Most of the objects I have photographed are made by hand, with older family members passing on their skills to the younger ones. Some things are used every day: brooms to clear the compounds, hats for working out in the hot sun, pestles and mortars for pounding up food—a sound heard before mealtimes even in the cities. Other things are brought out on special occasions, like the musical *ishaka*, and the colorful necklaces women wear for important village events.

In many parts of Africa, grandmothers play a vital family role helping to bring up the children. When children visit their grandparents, they are often given a present, perhaps of homegrown fruit and vegetables— and sometimes the children give a present in return. As Emeka daydreams of all the things he could take his grandmother, he shows just how much he loves her.

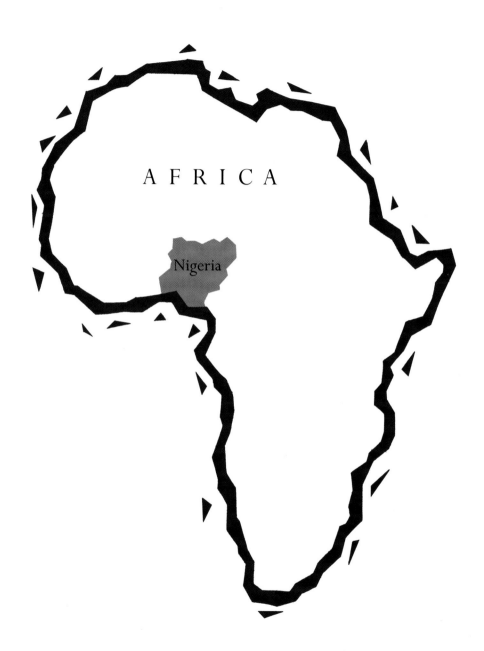

AFRICA

Nigeria

# 1

**One** boy who was not too small, but not too big either, set off to visit his grandmother in the next village. His name was Emeka.

## Okoso

Children play this game with spinning tops, empty snail shells—or anything that spins. These girls are playing with a used pen top. The player whose *okoso* spins the longest is the winner.

**2**

**Two** of Emeka's friends, Bola and Ada, were kneeling on the path playing *okoso*, his favorite game.

Emeka smiled as he passed them, but he didn't stop because he was thinking, "What can I take Granny as a present?"

# 3

**Three** women on their way to market turned to say hello to Emeka. "There must be lots of things in the market that Granny would like," he thought, walking that way too.

## Markets

Markets are important meeting places for people from villages all around. The local chief is always there to act as chief official. As well as buying food, clothes and household things, you can get your hair plaited and your bicycle repaired at the local market.

# 4

**Four** new brooms were propped up against a wall.

"Wouldn't it be nice if Granny had one of those," said Emeka, "for sweeping the leaves away that fall down from the orange and mango trees."

# 5

**Five** children dressed up in big grown-up hats smiled and waved at Emeka.

"What lovely hats!" he said. "Granny might like one of those to keep out the sun when she goes to the farm or to market."

# 6

**Six** beautiful beaded necklaces were set out on display.

"My sister Oge wears beads like those," said Emeka. "Granny might say, 'Child, I am far too old for necklaces!' but I think she would look just as lovely as Oge."

## Necklaces

Young women and babies wear them all the time, old women just for special occasions. Some necklaces are made from the dried seeds of the *akodegbe* plant, and some from glass or dyed rubber beads.

# 7

**Seven** musical instruments called *ishaka* caught Emeka's eye. Nearby, two girls were trying to play them like grown-up musicians.

Emeka laughed. "With those *ishaka,* Granny's dance group would be a big hit when they perform for the village."

## Ishaka

These musical instruments are made from natural or red-dyed gourds hung with dried seeds from the *akodegbe* plant, or from pieces of cooked, dyed rubber taken from the rubber tree. Shaken from side to side, they make a distinctive soft, rattling sound.

# 8

**Eight** water-pots, some tall, some small, stood on sale by the roadside. Emeka looked them up and down.

"With pots like those, Granny could store water for days and days, and give the garden plenty to drink. Then her tomatoes would grow bigger than ever."

## Water

In many African countries, the year is divided into rainy and dry seasons. People store water in earthenware pots, in plastic containers and in huge water tanks to use during the dry season, which lasts for several months.

# 9

**Nine** mortars and some pestles were lined up in rows at the end of the market.

"Some of those would be good for Granny's kitchen," thought Emeka. "Then, when I visit her with my cousins, we could help her to pound up yams for supper.

"But with no money, I can't give her anything." He walked slowly up to his grandmother's house.

## Pestles and mortars

Pestles and mortars are used for grinding up food. The wood-carver makes them from a tree trunk, hollowing out a piece very carefully to make the mortar. The pestle is shaped to make it easy to handle and to grind up different kinds of food.

**10**

**Ten** of Emeka's cousins were there, waiting to play with him. Emeka ran to tell his grandmother about all the things he wanted to bring her. But she just gave him a big hug, and said, "Child, you're the best present of all!"

## Families

In many parts of Africa, a typical family household includes three generations, and the doors are always open to aunts, uncles and cousins—so there is someone to look after the children when the parents are out.